Informing the legislative debate since 1914

Small Business: Access to Capital and Job Creation

Robert Jay Dilger

Senior Specialist in American National Government

February 18, 2014

Congressional Research Service

7-5700

www.crs.gov

R40985

Summary

The SBA administers several programs to support small businesses, including loan guaranty and venture capital programs to enhance small business access to capital; contracting programs to increase small business opportunities in federal contracting; direct loan programs for businesses, homeowners, and renters to assist their recovery from natural disasters; and small business management and technical assistance training programs to assist business formation and expansion. Congressional interest in these programs has increased in recent years, primarily because assisting small business is viewed as a means to enhance economic growth.

Some, including President Obama, have argued that the SBA should be provided additional resources to assist small businesses in acquiring capital necessary to start, continue, or expand operations and create jobs. Others worry about the long-term adverse economic effects of spending programs that increase the federal deficit. They advocate business tax reduction, reform of financial credit market regulation, and federal fiscal restraint as the best means to assist small business economic growth and job creation.

During the 111th Congress, several laws were enacted to enhance small business access to capital. For example, P.L. 111-5, the American Recovery and Reinvestment Act of 2009 (ARRA), provided the SBA an additional $730 million, including $375 million to temporarily subsidize SBA fees and increase the 7(a) loan guaranty program's maximum loan guaranty percentage to 90%. P.L. 111-240, the Small Business Jobs Act of 2010, authorized a $30 billion Small Business Lending Fund to encourage community banks to provide small business loans ($4 billion was issued), a $1.5 billion State Small Business Credit Initiative to provide funding to participating states with small business capital access programs, numerous changes to the SBA's loan guaranty and contracting programs, $510 million to continue the SBA's fee subsidies and 90% maximum loan guaranty percentage through December 31, 2010, and about $12 billion in tax relief for small businesses. The SBA subsequently was provided authority to continue the fee subsidies and the 90% maximum loan guaranty percentage through March 4, 2011, or until available funding was exhausted, which occurred on January 3, 2011.

During the 112th Congress, several bills were introduced to enhance small business access to capital, including bills to extend the SBA's temporary fee subsidies and the 90% maximum loan guaranty percentage. Congress did not adopt these legislative efforts. Instead, Congress passed legislation to enhance small business contracting opportunities, expand access to the SBA's surety bond guarantee program, amend the SBA's size standard practices, require a review and reassessment of the federal procurement small business goaling program, and expand small business mentor-protégé programs.

During the 113th Congress, P.L. 113-76, the Consolidated Appropriations Act, 2014, increased the annual authorization amount for the SBA's Small Business Investment Company venture capital program to $4 billion from $3 billion. The increased authorization amount is designed to provide small businesses additional access to venture capital.

This report addresses a core issue facing the 113th Congress: What, if any, additional action should the federal government take to enhance small business access to capital? After discussing the role of small business in job creation and retention, this report provides an assessment of the supply and demand for small business loans and recently enacted laws designed to enhance small business access to capital by either increasing the supply of small business loans or the demand for small business loans, or both. It also examines recent actions concerning the SBA's budget and concludes with a brief overview of three legislative options available to address small business access to capital issues during the 113th Congress: wait-and-see, enact additional programs, or reduce and consolidate existing programs.

Contents

Small Business Access to Capital 1
Three Indicators of the Supply and Demand for Private-Sector Small Business Loans 3
    Federal Reserve Board: Surveys of Senior Loan Officers 3
    FDIC Call Reports: Outstanding Small Business Loans 5
    Federal Reserve Board: Survey of Commercial Banks 6
SBA Lending 8
Recent Laws Designed to Enhance the Supply of Small Business Loans 12
Recent Laws Designed to Enhance the Demand for Small Business Loans 15
Discussion 18
SBA Funding 21
Concluding Observations 24

Figures

Figure 1. Small Business Lending Environment, 2000-2013 4
Figure 2. Outstanding Small Business Loans, Non-Agricultural Purposes, 2005-2013 6
Figure 3. Estimated Value of Commercial and Industrial Loans Made by Commercial
Banks on a Quarterly Basis, Including Loans Under $1 Million, 2005-2013 7

Tables

Table 1. Estimated Value of Commercial and Industrial Loans Made by Commercial
Banks, on an Annual Basis, 2005-2013 8
Table 2. Selected Small Business Administration Financial Statistics, FY2000-FY2013 9
Table 3. Small Business Administration Funding, FY2000-FY2014 23
Table A-1. Selected Provisions, the Small Business Jobs Act of 2010 27

Appendixes

Appendix. Selected Provisions in the Small Business Jobs Act of 2010 27

Contacts

Author Contact Information 29

Small Business Access to Capital

The Small Business Administration (SBA) administers several programs to support small businesses, including venture capital programs to provide "long-term loans and equity capital to small businesses, especially those with potential for substantial job growth and economic impact"[1] and loan guaranty programs to encourage lenders to provide loans to small businesses "that might not otherwise obtain financing on reasonable terms and conditions."[2] Historically, one of the justifications presented for funding the SBA's access to capital programs has been that small businesses can be at a disadvantage, compared with other businesses, when trying to obtain sufficient capital and credit.[3] As an economist explained:

> Growing firms need resources, but many small firms may have a hard time obtaining loans because they are young and have little credit history. Lenders may also be reluctant to lend to small firms with innovative products because it might be difficult to collect enough reliable information to correctly estimate the risk for such products. If it's true that the lending process leaves worthy projects unfunded, some suggest that it would be good to fix this "market failure" with government programs aimed at improving small businesses' access to credit.[4]

Congressional interest in the SBA's access to capital programs has increased in recent years, primarily because assisting small business in accessing capital is viewed as a means to enhance job creation and economic growth.[5]

Some, including President Obama, have argued that the SBA should be provided additional resources to assist small businesses in acquiring capital necessary to start, continue, or expand operations and create jobs. They note that small businesses have led job formation during previous economic recoveries.[6] In addition, the SBA has argued that "improving access to credit by small businesses is a crucial step in supporting economic recovery and job creation."[7]

---

[1] U.S. Small Business Administration, *Fiscal Year 2014 Congressional Budget Justification and FY2012 Annual Performance Report*, p. 58.

[2] U.S. Small Business Administration, *Fiscal Year 2010 Congressional Budget Justification*, p. 30.

[3] Proponents of providing federal funding for the SBA's loan guarantee programs also argue that small business can promote competitive markets. See P.L. 83-163, §2(a), as amended; and 15 U.S.C. §631a.

[4] Veronique de Rugy, *Why the Small Business Administration's Loan Programs Should Be Abolished*, American Enterprise Institute for Public Policy Research, AEI Working Paper #126, April 13, 2006, at http://www.aei.org/files/2006/04/13/20060414_wp126.pdf. Also, see U.S. Government Accountability Office, *Small Business Administration: 7(a) Loan Program Needs Additional Performance Measures*, GAO-08-226T, November 1, 2007, pp. 3, 9-11, at http://www.gao.gov/new.items/d08226t.pdf.

[5] For example, see The White House, "Remarks by the President on Job Creation and Economic Growth," December 8, 2009, at http://www.whitehouse.gov/the-press-office/remarks-president-job-creation-and-economic-growth; and U.S. Small Business Administration, *Fiscal Year 2014 Congressional Budget Justification and FY2012 Annual Performance Report*, pp. 1-14. For further analysis concerning the role of small business in job creation, see CRS Report R41392, *Small Business and the Expiration of the 2001 Tax Rate Reductions: Economic Issues*, by Jane G. Gravelle and Sean Lowry; and CRS Report R41523, *Small Business Administration and Job Creation*, by Robert Jay Dilger.

[6] U.S. Small Business Administration, Office of Advocacy, *Small Business Economic Indicators for 2003*, August 2004, p. 3; Brian Headd, "Small Businesses Most Likely to Lead Economic Recovery," *The Small Business Advocate*, vol. 28, no. 6 (July 2009), pp. 1, 2; and U.S. Small Business Administration, *FY2013 Congressional Budget Justification and FY2011 Annual Performance Report*, p. 1.

[7] U.S. Small Business Administration, "President Obama Announces New Efforts to Improve Access to Credit for Small Businesses," October 21, 2009, at http://www.whitehouse.gov/assets/documents/small_business_final.pdf.

Others worry about the long-term adverse economic effects of spending programs that increase the federal deficit. They advocate business tax reduction, reform of financial credit market regulation, and federal fiscal restraint as the best means to assist small business economic growth and job creation.[8]

Economists generally do not view job creation as a justification for providing federal assistance to small businesses. They argue that in the long term such assistance will likely reallocate jobs within the economy, not increase them. In their view, jobs arise primarily from the size of the labor force, which depends largely on population, demographics, and factors that affect the choice of home versus market production (e.g., the entry of women in the workforce). However, economic theory does suggest that increased federal spending may result in additional jobs in the short term. For example, the SBA reported in September 2010 that the $730 million in additional funding provided to the agency by P.L. 111-5, the American Recovery and Reinvestment Act of 2009 (ARRA), created or retained 785,955 jobs.[9]

As will be discussed, the tightening of private sector lending standards and the disruption of credit markets in 2008 and 2009 led to increased concern in Congress that small businesses might be prevented from accessing sufficient capital to start, continue, or expand their operations—actions that were expected to lead to higher levels of employment. As the SBA indicated in its FY2010 congressional budget justification report:

> Over the last decade, small businesses across this country have been responsible for the majority of new private sector jobs, leaving little doubt that they are a vital engine for the nation's economic growth. However, with the United States facing the most severe economic crisis in more than 70 years, small businesses are confronted with a frozen lending market and limited access to the capital they need to survive and grow at this critical time.[10]

Since then credit markets have improved and lending standards have moderated, but congressional concern about the economy and disagreements concerning the best means to enhance job creation and economic growth remain.

During the 111th Congress, several laws were enacted to enhance small business access to capital. For example, P.L. 111-5 provided the SBA an additional $730 million, including $375 million to temporarily subsidize SBA fees and increase the 7(a) loan guaranty program's maximum loan guaranty percentage to 90%. P.L. 111-240, the Small Business Jobs Act of 2010, authorized the Secretary of the Treasury to establish a $30 billion Small Business Lending Fund to encourage community banks to provide small business loans ($4 billion was issued), a $1.5 billion State Small Business Credit Initiative to provide funding to participating states with small business capital access programs, numerous changes to the SBA's loan guaranty and contracting programs, $510 million to continue the SBA's fee subsidies and the 7(a) program's 90% maximum loan guaranty percentage through December 31, 2010, and about $12 billion in tax relief for small

---

[8] Susan Eckerly, "NFIB Responds to President's Small Business Lending Initiatives," Washington, DC, October 21, 2009, at http://www.nfib.com/newsroom/newsroom-item/cmsid/50080/; NFIB, "Government Spending," Washington, DC, at http://www.nfib.com/issues-elections/issues-elections-item/cmsid/49051/; and National Federation of Independent Business, "Payroll Tax Holiday," at http://www.nfib.com/issues-elections/issues-elections-item/cmsid/49039/.

[9] U.S. Small Business Administration, "FY2009/2010 Final—Recovery Program Performance Report, September 2010," September, 2010, at http://archive.sba.gov/idc/groups/public/documents/sba_homepage/perform_report_9_2010.pdf.

[10] U.S. Small Business Administration, *Fiscal Year 2010 Congressional Budget Justification*, p. 1.

businesses (see the **Appendix** for a list of its key provisions). The SBA subsequently was provided authority to continue the fee subsidies and the 90% loan guaranty percentage through March 4, 2011, or until available funding was exhausted, which occurred on January 3, 2011.[11]

During the 112th Congress, several bills were introduced to enhance small business access to capital, including bills to extend the SBA's temporary fee subsidies and increase the 7(a) program's loan guaranty percentage to 90%.[12] Congress did not adopt these legislative efforts. Instead, Congress passed legislation designed to enhance small business contracting opportunities, expand access to the SBA's surety bond guarantee program, amend the SBA's size standard practices, require a review and reassessment of the federal procurement small business goaling program, and expand small business mentor-protégé programs.[13]

During the 113th Congress, P.L. 113-76, the Consolidated Appropriations Act, 2014, increased the annual authorization amount for the SBA's Small Business Investment Company venture capital program to $4 billion from $3 billion. As will be discussed, the increased authorization amount is designed to provide small businesses additional access to venture capital.

This report addresses a core issue facing the 113th Congress: What, if any, additional action should the federal government take to enhance small business access to capital? After discussing the role of small business in job creation and retention, this report provides an assessment of the supply and demand for small business loans, including the number and amount of small business loans guaranteed by the SBA. It also discusses several laws recently enacted by Congress to enhance small business access to capital by increasing the supply of small business loans or the demand for small business loans, or both. It also examines recent actions concerning the SBA's budget and concludes with a brief overview of three legislative options available to address small business access to capital issues during the 113th Congress: wait-and-see, enact additional programs, or reduce and consolidate existing programs.

Three Indicators of the Supply and Demand for Private-Sector Small Business Loans

Federal Reserve Board: Surveys of Senior Loan Officers

Each quarter, the Federal Reserve Board surveys senior loan officers concerning their bank's lending practices. The survey includes a question concerning their bank's credit standards for small business loans: "Over the past three months, how have your bank's credit standards for approving applications for C&I [commercial and industrial] loans or credit lines—other than those to be used to finance mergers and acquisitions—for small firms (annual sales of less than $50 million) changed?" The senior loan officers are asked to indicate if their bank's credit standards have "Tightened considerably," "Tightened somewhat," "Remained basically unchanged," "Eased somewhat," or "Eased considerably." Subtracting the percentage of

---

[11] P.L. 111-322, the Continuing Appropriations and Surface Transportation Extensions Act, 2011.

[12] For example, see H.R. 5851, the Increasing Small Business Lending Act of 2012 (112th Congress); and S. 1828, the Increasing Small Business Lending Act of 2011 (112th Congress).

[13] P.L. 112-239, the National Defense Authorization Act for Fiscal Year 2013.

respondents reporting "Eased somewhat" and "Eased considerably" from the percentage of respondents reporting "Tightened considerably" and "Tightened somewhat" provides an indication of the market's supply of small business loans.

As shown in **Figure 1**, senior loan officers reported that they tightened small business loan credit standards during the early 2000s; loosened them during the mid-2000s, and tightened them during the late 2000s. Since 2009, small business credit markets have improved, and most senior loan officers report that they are no longer tightening their small business lending standards.

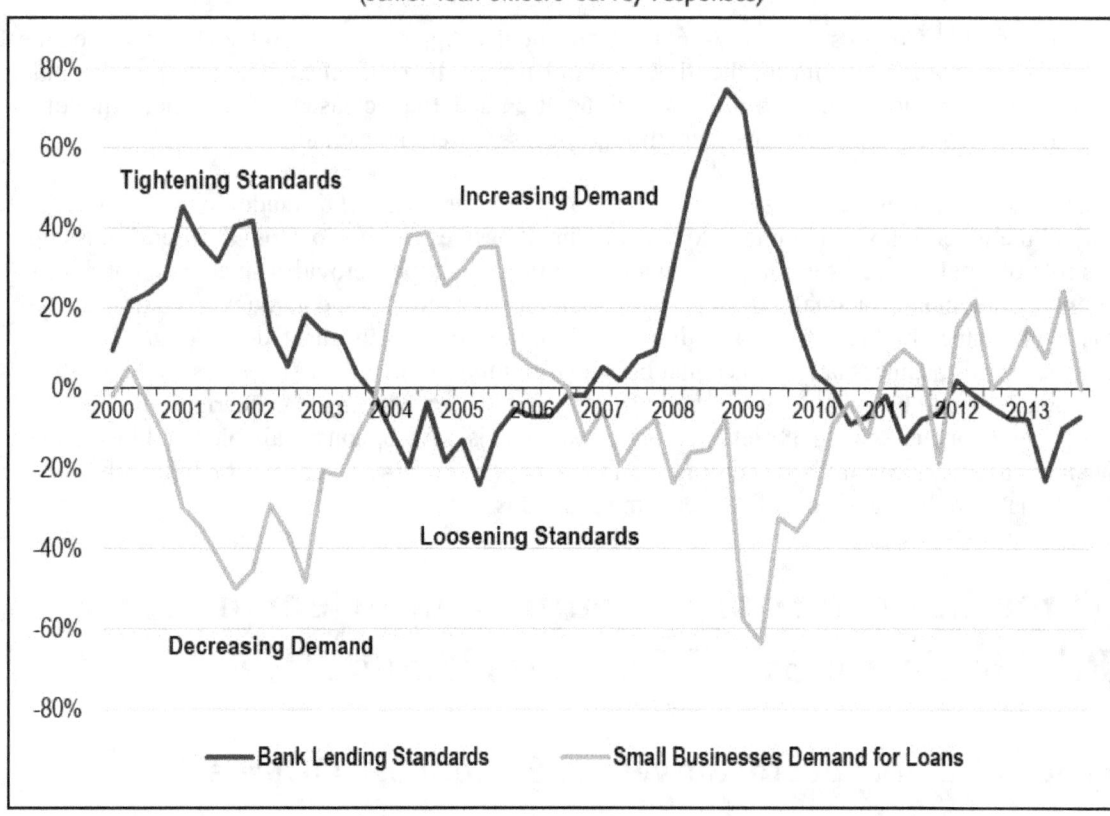

Figure 1. Small Business Lending Environment, 2000-2013
(senior loan officers' survey responses)

Source: Federal Reserve Board, "Senior Loan Officer Opinion Survey on Bank Lending Practices," at http://www.federalreserve.gov/boarddocs/SnLoanSurvey/; and Brian Headd, "Forum Seeks Solutions To Thaw Frozen Small Business Credit," *The Small Business Advocate*, vol. 28, no. 10 (December 2009), p. 3, at http://www.sba.gov/sites/default/files/The%20Small%20Business%20Advocate%20-%20December%202009.pdf.

The survey also includes a question concerning the demand for small business loans: "Apart from normal seasonal variation, how has demand for C&I loans changed over the past three months for small firms (annual sales of less than $50 million)?" Senior loan officers are asked to indicate if demand was "Substantially stronger," "Moderately stronger," "About the same," "Moderately weaker," or "Substantially weaker." Subtracting the percentage of respondents reporting "Moderately weaker" and "Substantially weaker" from the percentage of respondents reporting "Substantially stronger" and "Moderately stronger" provides an indication of the market's demand for small business loans.

As shown in **Figure 1**, senior loan officers reported that the demand for small business loans declined from 2000 to 2004, increased from 2004 to late 2006, declined somewhat in 2007 and 2008, and declined significantly in 2009. Demand then leveled off (at a relatively reduced level) during 2010, increased somewhat during the first half of 2011, declined somewhat during the latter half of 2011, and has increased somewhat since then.[14]

FDIC Call Reports: Outstanding Small Business Loans

The Federal Deposit Insurance Corporation (FDIC) reports bank lending statistics on a quarterly basis drawn from the banks' Consolidated Reports of Condition and Income (Call Report).[15] As shown in **Figure 2**, the combination of decreased supply and demand for small business loans over the past five years has led to a decline in the total amount of outstanding small business debt. Since peaking at $711.5 billion in the second quarter (June 30) of 2008, the FDIC reports that the total amount of outstanding, non-agricultural small business debt (defined by the FDIC as a loan of $1 million or less) declined to $695.2 billion in the second quarter of 2009, $652.2 billion in the second quarter of 2010, $607.6 billion in the second quarter of 2011, $587.8 billion in the second quarter of 2012, and $585.3 billion in the second quarter of 2013.[16]

---

[14] Federal Reserve Board, "Senior Loan Officer Opinion Survey on Bank Lending Practices," at http://www.federalreserve.gov/boarddocs/SnLoanSurvey/.

[15] Every national bank, state member bank, and insured nonmember bank is required by its primary federal regulator to file consolidated Reports of Condition and Income as of the close of business on the last day of each calendar quarter (the report date). The specific reporting requirements depend upon the size of the bank and whether it has any foreign offices.

[16] Federal Deposit Insurance Corporation, "Statistics on Depository Institutions," at http://www2.fdic.gov/SDI/main.asp.

Figure 2. Outstanding Small Business Loans, Non-Agricultural Purposes, 2005-2013
(billions of $)

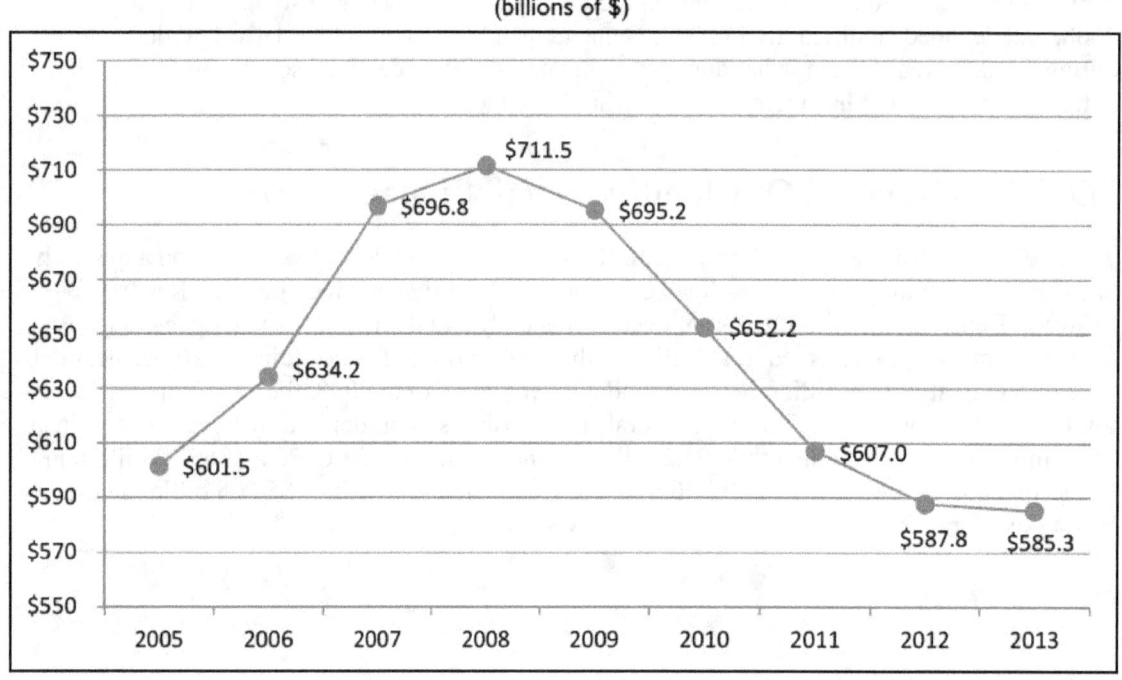

Source: Federal Deposit Insurance Corporation, "Statistics on Depository Institutions," at http://www2.fdic.gov/SDI/main.asp.

Notes: Data as of June 30th each year. The FDIC defines a small business loan as a loan of $1 million or less.

A declining amount of small business outstanding debt does not necessarily mean that the supply of small business loans is declining. However, many, including the SBA, view the decline in small business outstanding debt as a signal that small businesses might be experiencing difficulties in accessing sufficient capital to enable them to lead job growth during the current recovery.

Federal Reserve Board: Survey of Commercial Banks

The Federal Reserve Board conducts a quarterly "Survey of Terms of Business Lending" which provides information concerning the lending activity of commercial banks.[17] As shown in **Figure 3**, the Federal Reserve Board data indicate that the total estimated value of commercial and industrial loans (hereafter C&I loans) provided by commercial banks has experienced some volatility over the years. For example, the total estimated value of commercial banks' C&I loans fell during all four quarters in 2009 and the first quarter in 2010, and, with some declines, has been generally increasing since then.

---

[17] The Survey of Terms of Business Lending collects data on gross loan extensions made during the first full business week in the middle month of each quarter. The authorized panel size for the survey is 348 domestically chartered commercial banks and 50 U.S. branches and agencies of foreign banks. The sample data are used to estimate the terms of loans extended during that week at all domestic commercial banks and all U.S. branches and agencies of foreign banks. See Board of Governors of the Federal Reserve System, "Survey of Terms of Business Lending - E.2, November 4-8, 2013," at http://www.federalreserve.gov/releases/E2/current/default.htm.

The data also indicate that the estimated value of commercial banks' small business loans (defined by the Federal Reserve Board as a C&I loan under $1 million) has been somewhat less volatile, ranging from a high of $15.9 billion in the second quarter of 2006 to a low of $10.0 billion in the third quarter of 2009. During the fourth quarter of 2013, the estimated value of commercial banks' small business loans was $14.8 billion.

Figure 3. Estimated Value of Commercial and Industrial Loans Made by Commercial Banks on a Quarterly Basis, Including Loans Under $1 Million, 2005-2013

(billions of $)

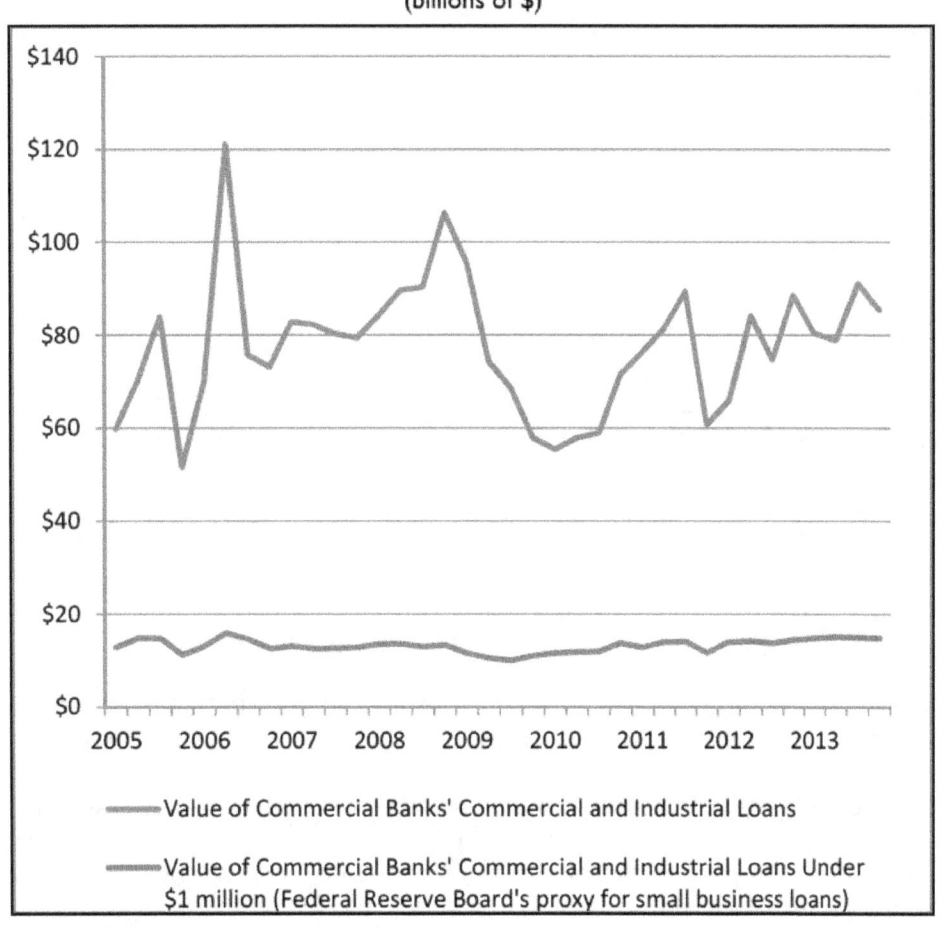

Source: Board of Governors of the Federal Reserve System, "Survey of Terms of Business Lending - E.2," at http://www.federalreserve.gov/releases/E2/default.htm.

Notes: Data was collected during the first full business week in the middle month of each quarter. Value is the amount borrowed.

Table 1 shows the estimated total value of commercial and industrial loans made by commercial banks, the estimated value of commercial and industrial loans they made in loans under $1 million (the Federal Reserve Board's proxy for small business loans), and the percentage of the estimated total value of commercial and industrial loans they made in loans under $1 million on an annualized basis for 2005 through 2013.

Table 1. Estimated Value of Commercial and Industrial Loans Made by Commercial Banks, on an Annual Basis, 2005-2013

(billions of $)

Calendar Year	Estimated Total Value of Commercial and Industrial Loans Made by Commercial Banks	Estimated Value of Commercial and Industrial Loans Made by Commercial Banks Under $1 Million	% of Estimated Total Value of Commercial and Industrial Loans Made by Commercial Banks Under $1 Million
2013	$335.7	$59.7	17.8%
2012	$313.3	$56.5	18.0%
2011	$308.1	$52.6	17.1%
2010	$244.0	$49.1	20.1%
2009	$296.4	$43.1	14.5%
2008	$370.7	$53.4	14.4%
2007	$324.8	$51.2	15.8%
2006	$339.7	$56.1	16.5%
2005	$265.6	$53.6	20.2%
Total	$2,798.3	$475.3	17.0%

Source: Board of Governors of the Federal Reserve System, "Survey of Terms of Business Lending - E.2," at http://www.federalreserve.gov/releases/E2/default.htm.

Notes: Data was collected during the first full business week in the middle month of each quarter and summed to provide annual data. Value is the amount borrowed.

SBA Lending

Table 2 shows selected financial statistics for the SBA from FY2000 to FY2013. It provides an overview of the extent of the SBA's various programs to enhance small business access to capital.

The first two columns report the amount and number of non-disaster small business loans guaranteed by the SBA. The figures reflect loans that were disbursed and are less than the amount and number of loans approved by the SBA. Each year, 7% to 10% of the loans approved by the SBA are subsequently canceled for a variety of reasons, typically by the borrower.

The third column reports the number of bonds guaranteed under the SBA's surety bond guarantee program.[18] A surety bond is a three-party instrument between a surety (someone who agrees to be responsible for the debt or obligation of another), a contractor, and a project owner. The agreement binds the contractor to comply with the contract's terms and conditions. If the contractor is unable to successfully perform the contract, the surety assumes the contractor's responsibilities and ensures that the project is completed. It is designed to reduce the risk of contracting with small businesses that may not have the credit history or prior experience of larger businesses. The SBA does not issue surety bonds. Instead, it provides and manages surety

---

[18] For further information and analysis of the SBA's surety bond guarantee program, see CRS Report R42037, *SBA Surety Bond Guarantee Program*, by Robert Jay Dilger.

bond guarantees for qualified small and emerging businesses through its Surety Bond Guarantee (SBG) Program. The SBA reimburses a participating surety (within specified limits) for losses incurred due to a contractor's default on a bond.[19]

The fourth column reports the outstanding principal balance for the SBA's 7(a) secondary market guarantee program, which is discussed later in this report. The final column reports the SBA's outstanding principal balance of loans that have not been charged off as of the end of the fiscal year. It provides a measure of the SBA's scope of lending.

Table 2. Selected Small Business Administration Financial Statistics, FY2000-FY2013

($ in millions)

Fiscal Year	SBA Business Loan Guarantees		Surety Bond Guarantees Number	7(a) Secondary Market Guarantee Program Outstanding Principal	Unpaid Principal Loan Balance[b]
	Amount Disbursed[a]	Number Disbursed			
2013	$20,360	32,581	6,151	$20,500	$109,758
2012	$18,254	43,217	9,503	$19,200	$104,443
2011	$19,394	51,681	8,638	$17,600	$99,704
2010	$14,828	46,479	8,348	$15,500	$93,519
2009	$12,486	42,236	6,135	$14,700	$90,454
2008	$18,415	69,152	6,055	$14,900	$88,244
2007	$19,106	97,448	5,809	$14,100	$84,522
2006	$18,845	95,045	5,214	$14,600	$78,119
2005	$18,666	89,176	5,678	$14,900	$71,497
2004	$15,384	78,387	7,803	$14,100	$64,362
2003	$13,284	65,055	8,974	$13,000	$59,181
2002	$12,852	49,897	7,372	$12,000	$56,219
2001	$11,246	41,904	6,320	$11,000	$53,116
2000	$12,232	41,514	7,034	$10,000	$52,227

Sources: U.S. Small Business Administration, correspondence with the author, November 21, 2013 (loan guarantees); U.S. Small Business Administration, *Agency Financial Report [various fiscal years]* (surety bonds and 7(a) secondary market guarantee program outstanding principal); and U.S. Small Business Administration, "Unpaid Principal Balance," at http://www.sba.gov/sites/default/files/files/WDS_Table1_UPB_Report(3).pdf.

a. The amount disbursed is the amount provided to the borrower. In recent years, the SBA has guaranteed about 84% to 87% of the loan amount approved.

b. Includes unpaid principal loan balance for disaster loans: $5.8 billion in FY2000, $4.3 billion in FY2001, $3.6 billion in FY2002, $2.9 billion in FY2003, $3.0 billion in FY2004, $3.6 billion in FY2005, $6.8 billion in

---

[19] U.S. Small Business Administration, "Surety Bonds," at http://www.sba.gov/category/navigation-structure/loans-grants/bonds/surety-bonds.

FY2006, $9.0 billion in FY2007, $8.6 billion in FY2008, $8.4 billion in FY2009, $7.9 billion in FY2010, $7.5 billion in FY2011, $7.2 billion in FY2012, and $7.2 billion in FY2013.

As shown in **Table 2**, the amount of non-disaster small business loans disbursed by the SBA declined in FY2008 and FY2009; increased, but remained below pre-recession levels in FY2010; and returned to pre-recession levels in FY2011, FY2012, and FY2013.[20]

The decline in the amount of small business loans guaranteed by the SBA during FY2008 and FY2009 was, at least in part, due to three interrelated factors. First, many lending institutions become increasingly reluctant to lend to small businesses, even with an SBA loan guarantee. As loan defaults increased due to the recession, earnings fell and an increasing number of lending institutions failed.[21] For example, three lending institutions failed in 2007. That number increased to 26 in 2008 and to 140 in 2009.[22] Included in the list of failed lending institutions in 2009 was CIT Group, Inc., the nation's largest lender to small businesses.[23] When lending institutions anticipate difficulty in making a profit, are losing money, or have diminished expectations of future profits, they tend to become more risk averse and the supply of business loans, including small business loans, tends to decline.

Second, the secondary market for small business loans, as with other secondary markets, began to contract in October 2008, reached its nadir in January 2009, and then began a relatively prolonged recovery.[24] In a secondary market, loans are pooled together and packaged as securities for sale to investors. This practice makes more capital available by allowing lending institutions to remove existing loans from their balance sheets, freeing them to make new loans.[25] When secondary credit markets constrict, lenders tend to become both less willing and less able to supply small business loans. For example, the secondary market volume for SBA 7(a) loans averaged $328 million a month from January 2008 through September 2008, and then fell each

---

[20] The recession began in December 2007 and ended in June 2009.

[21] FDIC-insured lending institutions lost $12.9 billion in 2008, including a $37.8 billion loss in the fourth quarter, which more than erased $24.9 billion in profits during the previous three quarters. In 2009, FDIC-insured lending institutions had a net profit of $4.2 billion. See Federal Deposit Insurance Corporation, "Quarterly Banking Profile: Quarterly Net Income," at http://www2.fdic.gov/qbp/2009dec/chart1.htm. In 2010, FDIC-insured lending institutions had $85.4 billion in net profits. See Federal Deposit Insurance Corporation, "Quarterly Banking Profile: Quarterly Net Income," at http://www2.fdic.gov/qbp/2010dec/chart1.htm.

[22] The number of lending institutions which failed increased to 157 in 2010. In 2011, 92 lending institutions failed and in 2012 92 lending institutions failed. See Federal Deposit Insurance Corporation, "Failed Bank List," at http://www.fdic.gov/bank/individual/failed/banklist.html.

[23] Patrice Hill, "Lender to small business bankrupt," *The Washington Post*, November 2, 2009, pp. A1, A10. CIT Group, Inc. failed on November 1, 2009.

[24] The Federal Reserve Bank of New York, using authority provided under §13(3) of the Federal Reserve Act, created the Term Asset-Backed Securities Loan Facility (TALF) on March 3, 2009, to stabilize secondary credit markets by lending up to $200 billion to eligible owners of certain AAA-rated asset backed securities (ABS) backed by newly and recently originated auto loans, credit card loans, student loans, and SBA-guaranteed small business loans. The initial TALF subscription took place on March 19, 2009, and the last one took place in June 2010. There were 23 monthly ABS and Commercial Mortgage Backed Securities (CMBS) subscriptions. TALF supported about $58 billion of ABS and $12 billion of CMBS. See Federal Reserve Bank of New York, "Term Asset-Backed Securities Loan Facility: Terms and Conditions," New York, NY, at http://www.newyorkfed.org/markets/talf_terms.html; Federal Reserve Bank of New York, "New York Fed releases revised TALF Master Loan and Security Agreement and appendices," press release, New York, NY, at http://www.federalreserve.gov/newsevents/press/monetary/20090303a.htm; and U.S. Department of the Treasury, "Secretary of the Treasury Timothy F. Geithner, Written Testimony Congressional Oversight Panel," press release, June 22, 2010, at http://cop.senate.gov/documents/testimony-062210-geithner.pdf.

[25] U.S. Small Business Administration, Office of Advocacy, *An Exploration of a Secondary Market for Small Business Loans*, April 2003, p. 1, at http://archive.sba.gov/advo/research/rs227_tot.pdf.

succeeding month, declining to under $100 million in January 2009.[26] The SBA estimates that about half of the lenders that make SBA guaranteed loans resell them to obtain additional capital to make additional loans.

Third, the demand for small business loans declined. The SBA estimated that about 60% of the jobs lost in 2008 through the second quarter of 2009 were lost in small firms.[27] Monthly business surveys conducted by Automatic Data Processing, Inc. (ADP) suggest that about 81% of the 7.5 million jobs lost during the recession were in firms with less than 500 employees.[28] When business is slow, or when expectations of business sales growth are diminished, business owners (and entrepreneurs considering starting a new small business) tend to become more risk averse and the demand for small business loans tends to decline.

In 2009, the number and amount of small business loans guaranteed by the SBA declined sharply early in the year, followed by modest increases during the second and third quarters, and briefly surpassed pre-recession levels in the fourth quarter as small business owners took advantage of ARRA funded fee subsidies for the SBA's 7(a) and 504/CDC loan guaranty programs and an increase in the 7(a) program's maximum loan guaranty percentage to 90% which were expected to end by the end of the year.[29]

The SBA argued that the increase in the number and amount of small business loans it guaranteed during FY2010 was primarily due to fee subsidies and loan enhancements first put in place under ARRA and later extended by law to cover most of the fiscal year.[30] The SBA noted that its average weekly loan volume for FY2010 ($333 million) was 29% higher than its average weekly loan volume for FY2009 ($258 million).[31] Another likely factor contributing to the higher loan volume was a general improvement in the economy as the recession ended (officially in June 2009) and the economic recovery began, albeit slowly in many parts of the nation.

The demand for SBA loans increased significantly during the first quarter of FY2011 (October-December 2010), as borrowers took advantage of SBA fee subsidies that were expected to expire at the end of the calendar year. The SBA announced, on January 3, 2011, that it "approved nearly 22,000 small business loans for $10.47 billion, supporting a total of $12.16 billion in lending" during the first quarter of FY2011, which "was the highest volume in a fiscal year's first quarter than at any time in the agency's history."[32] After the fee subsidies ended, SBA lending declined

---

[26] U.S. Small Business Administration, "Six-Month Recovery Act Report Card," August 2009.

[27] Brian Headd, U.S. Small Business Administration, Office of Advocacy, "An Analysis of Small Business and Jobs," March 2010, p. 14, at http://www.sba.gov/sites/default/files/files/an%20analysis%20of%20small%20business%20and%20jobs(1).pdf.

[28] Automatic Data Processing, Inc. (ADP), "National Employment Report, December 2007," Roseland, NJ, p. 2, at http://www.adpemploymentreport.com/pdf/FINAL_Report_DEC_07.pdf; and ADP, "National Employment Report, September 2009," Roseland, NJ, p. 2, at http://www.adpemploymentreport.com/PDF/FINAL_Report_September_09.pdf.

[29] U.S. Small Business Administration, "Recovery Act Changes to SBA Loan Programs Sparked Major Mid-Year Turn-Around in Volume," October 1, 2009; and Nancy Waitz, "U.S. stimulus funds run out for lower SBA loan fees," Reuters News, November 24, 2009, at http://www.reuters.com/article/companyNewsAndPR/idUSN2431964620091125.

[30] U.S. Small Business Administration, "Recovery Loan Incentives Spurred Continued Rebound in SBA Lending in FY2010," October 4, 2010, at http://archive.sba.gov/idc/groups/public/documents/sba_homepage/news_release_10-54.pdf.

[31] Ibid.

[32] U.S. Small Business Administration, "Jobs Act Supported More Than $12 Billion in SBA Lending to Small (continued...)

during the second quarter of FY2011, and then increased somewhat during the final two quarters of FY2011. As mentioned previously, the amount of non-disaster small business loans disbursed by the SBA has continued at or above pre-recession levels since FY2011.

Recent Laws Designed to Enhance the Supply of Small Business Loans

As mentioned previously, several laws were enacted during the 110th and 111th Congresses to enhance small business access to capital. The following laws were enacted largely in response to the contraction of financial credit markets which started in 2008, and reached its nadir in early 2009.

P.L. 110-343, the Emergency Economic Stabilization Act of 2008, was designed to enhance the supply of loans to businesses of all sizes. The act authorized the Troubled Asset Relief Program (TARP) to "restore liquidity and stability to the financial system of the United States" by purchasing or insuring up to $700 billion in troubled assets from banks and other financial institutions.[33] TARP's purchase authority was later reduced from $700 billion to $475 billion by P.L. 111-203, the Dodd-Frank Wall Street Reform and Consumer Protection Act. The Department of the Treasury has disbursed $389 billion in TARP funds, including $337 million to purchase SBA 7(a) loan guaranty program securities.[34] The authority to make new TARP commitments expired on October 3, 2010.

P.L. 111-5, the American Recovery and Reinvestment Act of 2009 (ARRA), included several provisions to enhance the supply of loans to small businesses.[35] ARRA

- authorized the SBA to establish a temporary secondary market guarantee authority to provide a federal guarantee for pools of first lien 504/CDC program loans that are to be sold to third-party investors. The SBA was granted emergency rulemaking authority to issue regulations for the program within 15 days after enactment (by March 4, 2009). After experiencing unanticipated delays

---

(...continued)
Businesses in Just Three Months," January 3, 2011, at http://www.sba.gov/content/jobs-act-supported-more-12-billion-sba-lending-small-businesses-just-three-months.

[33] For further analysis, see CRS Report R41427, *Troubled Asset Relief Program (TARP): Implementation and Status*, by Baird Webel.

[34] U.S. Department of the Treasury, *Troubled Assets Relief Program Monthly 105(a) Report—November 2010*, December 10, 2010, pp. 2-4, at http://www.financialstability.gov/docs/November%20105(a)%20FINAL.pdf. On March 16, 2009, President Obama announced that the Department of the Treasury would use TARP funds to purchase up to $15 billion of SBA-guaranteed loans to "immediately unfreeze the secondary market for SBA loans and increase the liquidity of community banks." The plan was deferred after it met resistance from lenders. Some lenders objected to TARP's requirement that participating lenders comply with executive compensation limits and issue warrants to the federal government. Smaller, community banks objected to the program's paperwork requirements, such as the provision of a small-business lending plan and quarterly reports. See The White House, "Remarks by the President to Small Business Owners, Community Leaders, and Members of Congress," March 16, 2009, at http://www.whitehouse.gov/the_press_office/Remarks-by-the-President-to-small-business-owners/.

[35] For further analysis, see CRS Report R40728, *Small Business Tax Benefits and the American Recovery and Reinvestment Act of 2009*, by Gary Guenther and CRS Report R41385, *Small Business Legislation During the 111th Congress*, by Robert Jay Dilger and Gary Guenther.

in implementing the program due to "limited staff resources" and determining how to meet ARRA reporting requirements, the SBA issued regulations for its 504/CDC First Mortgage Loan Pooling program on October 30, 2009, and it became operational in June 2010.[36] The program was scheduled to end on February 16, 2011, or until $3 billion in new pools are created, whichever occurred first. As will be discussed, the Small Business Jobs Act of 2010 extended the program.[37]

- authorized the SBA to use emergency rulemaking authority to issue regulations within 30 days after enactment (by March 19, 2009), to make below market interest rate direct loans to SBA-designated "Systemically Important Secondary Market (SISM) Broker-Dealers." These broker-dealers would use the loan funds to purchase SBA-guaranteed loans from commercial lenders, assemble them into pools, and sell them to investors in the secondary loan market. The SBA experienced unanticipated delays in implementing the program primarily due to the need to determine "the extent to which broker-dealers, and perhaps small business lenders, would be required to share in the potential losses associated with extending the guarantee in the 504 loan program."[38] The SBA issued regulations to establish the Direct Loan Program for Systemically Important Secondary Market Broker-Dealers on November 19, 2009.[39]

- provided $255 million for a temporary, two-year small business stabilization program to guarantee loans of $35,000 or less to small businesses for qualified debt consolidation, later named the America's Recovery Capital (ARC) Loan program (the program ceased issuing new loan guarantees on September 30, 2010); $15 million for the SBA's surety bond program, and temporarily increased the maximum bond amount from $2 million to $5 million, and up to $10 million under certain conditions (the higher maximum bond amounts ended on September 30, 2010); $6 million for the SBA's Microloan program's lending program and $24 million for the Microloan program's technical assistance program; and increased the funds ("leverage") available to SBA-licensed Small Business Investment Companies (SBICs) to no more than 300% of the company's private capital or $150,000,000, whichever is less.

---

[36] U.S. Small Business Administration, "SBA Creates Secondary Market Guarantee Program for 504 First Mortgage Loan Pools," October 28, 2009; U.S. Government Accountability Office, *Recovery Act: Project Selection and Starts Are Influenced by Certain Federal Requirements and Other Factors*, GAO-10-383, February 10, 2010, p. 23, at http://www.gao.gov/new.items/d10383.pdf; and U.S. Small Business Administration, "New First Mortgage Loan Poolers Will Jump-Start Secondary Market for SBA 504 Loans, Make Credit More Available," June 24, 2010, at http://www.sba.gov/about-sba-services/7367/5728.

[37] U.S. Small Business Administration, "The American Recovery and Reinvestment Act of 2009: Secondary Market First Lien Position 504 Loan Pool Guarantee," 74 *Federal Register* 56087, October 30, 2009; and U.S. Small Business Administration, "New First Mortgage Loan Poolers Will Jump-Start Secondary Market for SBA 504 Loans, Make Credit More Available, June 24, 2010, at http://www.sba.gov/about-sba-services/7367/5728.

[38] U.S. Government Accountability Office, Status of the Small Business Administration's Implementation of Administrative Provisions in the American Recovery and Reinvestment Act of 2009, GAO-10-298R, January 19, 2010, p. 7, at http://www.gao.gov/new.items/d10298r.pdf.

[39] U.S. Small Business Administration, "American Recovery and Reinvestment Act: Loan Program for Systemically Important SBA Secondary Market Broker-Dealers," 74 *Federal Register* 59891, November 19, 2009.

- authorized the SBA to guarantee 504/CDC loans used to refinance business expansion projects as long as the existing indebtedness did not exceed 50% of the project cost of the expansion and the borrower met specified requirements.

P.L. 111-240, the Small Business Jobs Act of 2010, was enacted after the financial credit markets had stabilized. It included several provisions designed to enhance the supply of loans to small businesses. For example, the act

- authorized the Secretary of the Treasury to establish a $30 billion Small Business Lending Fund (SBLF) to encourage community banks to provide small business loans ($4 billion was issued) and a $1.5 billion State Small Business Credit Initiative (SSBCI) to provide funding to participating states with small business capital access programs.[40]

- extended the SBA's secondary market guarantee authority from two years after the date of ARRA's enactment to two years after the date of the program's first sale of a pool of first lien position 504/CDC loans to a third-party investor (which took place on September 24, 2010).[41]

- authorized $22.5 million for a temporary, three-year Small Business Intermediary Lending Pilot Program to provide direct loans to intermediaries which provide loans to small business startups, newly established small businesses, and growing small businesses. On August 4, 2011, the SBA announced the first 20 community lenders which were selected to participate in the program.[42]

- authorized $15 million in additional funding for the SBA's 7(a) loan guaranty program.

- increased the loan guarantee limits for the SBA's 7(a) program from $2 million to $5 million, and for the 504/CDC program from $1.5 million to $5 million for "regular" borrowers, from $2 million to $5 million if the loan proceeds are directed toward one or more specified public policy goals, and from $4 million to $5.5 million for manufacturers.

- increased the SBA's Microloan program's loan limit for borrowers from $35,000 to $50,000 and for microlender intermediaries after their first year in the program from $3.5 million to $5 million.[43]

---

[40] For further analysis of the Small Business Lending Fund, see CRS Report R42045, *The Small Business Lending Fund*, by Robert Jay Dilger. For a further analysis of the State Small Business Credit Initiative see CRS Report R42581, *State Small Business Credit Initiative: Implementation and Funding Issues*, by Robert Jay Dilger.

[41] U.S. Small Business Administration, Office of Congressional and Legislative Affairs, correspondence with the author, January 4, 2010.

[42] U.S. Small Business Administration, "Small Businesses Have New Non-Profit Sources for SBA-financed Loans," August 4, 2011, at http://www.sba.gov/content/intermediary-lending-pilot-program-0.

[43] The act also temporarily allowed the SBA to waive, in whole or in part, for successive fiscal years, the non-federal share requirement for loans to the Microloan program's intermediaries and for grants made to Microloan intermediaries for small business marketing, management, and technical assistance under specified circumstances (e.g., the economic conditions affecting the intermediary). See P.L. 111-240, the Small Business Jobs Act of 2010, §1401. Matching Requirements Under Small Business Programs.

- temporarily increased for one year the SBA 7(a) Express Program's loan limit from $350,000 to $1 million (the temporary increase expired on September 26, 2011).
- required the SBA to establish an on-line lending platform listing all SBA lenders and information concerning their loan rates.
- authorized the SBA to temporarily guarantee for two years, under specified circumstances, 504/CDC loans that refinance existing business debt even if the project does not involve the expansion of the business.

For additional details concerning provisions in the Small Business Jobs Act of 2010, see **Table A-1** in the **Appendix**.

During the 113th Congress, P.L. 113-76, the Consolidated Appropriations Act, 2014, included a provision increasing the annual authorization amount for the SBA's Small Business Investment Company (SBIC) program to $4 billion from $3 billion. The SBIC program is designed to "improve and stimulate the national economy in general and the small business segment thereof in particular" by stimulating and supplementing "the flow of private equity capital and long term loan funds which small business concerns need for the sound financing of their business operations and for their growth, expansion, and modernization, and which are not available in adequate supply."[44]

As of December 31, 2013, there were 287 privately owned and managed SBA-licensed SBICs providing small businesses private capital the SBIC has raised (called regulatory capital) and funds the SBIC borrows at favorable rates (called leverage) because the SBA guarantees the debenture (loan obligation). SBICs provide equity capital to small businesses in various ways, including by purchasing small business equity securities (e.g., stock, stock options, warrants, etc.), making loans to small businesses, purchasing debt securities from small businesses, and providing small businesses, subject to limitations, a guarantee of their monetary obligations to creditors not associated with the SBIC.[45]

In FY2013, the SBA committed to guarantee $2.15 billion in SBIC small business investments, and SBICs invested another $1.34 billion from private capital, for almost $3.5 billion in financing for 1,068 small businesses. Although the SBA's commitment of $2.15 billion in SBIC leverage in FY2013 was well below the new $4 billion threshold amount, advocates of the higher threshold argued that the increase would enable the program to grow, providing more capital to a larger number of small businesses in the future.

Recent Laws Designed to Enhance the Demand for Small Business Loans

ARRA provided the SBA $375 million to subsidize fees for the SBA's 7(a) and 504/CDC loan guaranty programs and to increase the 7(a) program's maximum loan guaranty percentage from

---

[44] 15 U.S.C. §661. For further information and analysis concerning the SBA's Small Business Investment Company program, see CRS Report R41456, *SBA Small Business Investment Company Program*, by Robert Jay Dilger.
[45] 13 CFR §107.820.

up to 85% of loans of $150,000 or less and up to 75% of loans exceeding $150,000 to 90% for all regular 7(a) loans through September 30, 2010, or when appropriated funding for the subsidies and loan modification was exhausted. The fee subsidies were designed to increase the demand for SBA loans by reducing loan costs.

ARRA's funding for the fee subsidies and 90% maximum loan guaranty percentage was about to be exhausted in November 2009, when Congress passed the first of six laws to extend the loan subsidies and 90% maximum loan guaranty percentage:

- P.L. 111-118, the Department of Defense Appropriations Act, 2010, provided the SBA $125 million to continue the fee subsides and 90% maximum loan guaranty percentage through February 28, 2010.

- P.L. 111-144, the Temporary Extension Act of 2010, provided the SBA $60 million to continue the fee subsides and 90% maximum loan guaranty percentage through March 28, 2010.

- P.L. 111-150, an act to extend the Small Business Loan Guarantee Program, and for other purposes, provided the SBA authority to reprogram $40 million in previously appropriated funds to continue the fee subsides and 90% maximum loan guaranty percentage through April 30, 2010.

- P.L. 111-157, the Continuing Extension Act of 2010, provided the SBA $80 million to continue the SBA's fee subsides and 90% maximum loan guaranty percentage through May 31, 2010.

- P.L. 111-240, the Small Business Jobs Act of 2010, provided $505 million (plus an additional $5 million for administrative expenses) to continue the SBA's fee subsides and 90% maximum loan guaranty percentage from the act's date of enactment (September 27, 2010) through December 31, 2010.

- P.L. 111-322, the Continuing Appropriations and Surface Transportation Extensions Act, 2011, authorizes the SBA to use funds provided under the Small Business Jobs Act of 2010 to continue the SBA's fee subsides and 90% maximum loan guaranty percentage through March 4, 2011, or until available funding is exhausted.

On January 3, 2011, the SBA announced that funding for the fee subsidies and 90% maximum loan guaranty percentage had been exhausted.[46]

ARRA also included 11 tax relief provisions that have the potential to benefit small businesses in a broad range of industries.[47] By reducing costs, it could be argued that providing tax relief for small businesses may lead to increased demand for small business loans because small business owners have additional resources available to invest in their business. The following five ARRA tax provisions provided about $5.7 billion in tax relief and were targeted at small businesses, whereas the other ARRA tax provisions were available to businesses of all sizes:

---

[46] U.S. Small Business Administration, "Jobs Act Supported More Than $12 Billion in SBA Lending to Small Businesses in Just Three Months," January 3, 2011, at http://www.sba.gov/content/jobs-act-supported-more-12-billion-sba-lending-small-businesses-just-three-months.

[47] For further analysis see CRS Report R40728, *Small Business Tax Benefits and the American Recovery and Reinvestment Act of 2009*, by Gary Guenther.

- allowed businesses with $15 million or less in average annual gross receipts in the past three years to carry back net operating losses from 2008 for up to five years instead of two years.
- extended through 2009 the enhanced expensing allowance, which allows businesses to deduct up to $250,000 of the cost of eligible assets placed in service in 2009, within certain limits.
- increased the exclusion of the gain on the sale of small business stock to 75% (instead of 50%) of any gain realized on the sale of eligible small business stock acquired between February 18, 2009, and December 31, 2010.
- reduced the recognition period from 10 years to seven years for corporate tax on sale of appreciated assets in 2009 or 2010 by S corporations that once were organized as C corporations.
- allowed individuals who had an adjusted gross income in 2008 of less than $500,000 and can prove that over half their income came from a small business to base their estimated tax payments for 2009 on 90% of their tax liability for 2008.

The Small Business Jobs Act of 2010 was designed to increase the demand for SBA loans by providing $505 million (plus an additional $5 million for related administrative expenses) to temporarily subsidize SBA's fees and increase the 7(a) program's maximum loan guaranty percentage to 90%. The act also required the SBA to establish an alternative size standard for the SBA's 7(a) and 504/CDC loan guaranty programs that uses maximum net worth and average net income as an alternative to the use of industry standards. It also established the following interim alternative size standard for both the 7(a) and 504/CDC programs: the business qualifies as small if it does not have a tangible net worth in excess of $15 million and does not have an average net income after federal taxes (excluding any carry-over losses) in excess of $5 million for two full fiscal years before the date of application. These changes were designed to increase the demand for small business loans by increasing the number of small businesses that are eligible for SBA assistance.[48]

The Small Business Jobs Act of 2010 also provided small businesses with about $12 billion in tax relief. The act

- raised the exclusion of gains on the sale or exchange of qualified small business stock from the federal income tax to 100%, with the full exclusion applying only to stock acquired the day after the date of enactment through the end of 2010;
- increased the deduction for qualified start-up expenditures from $5,000 to $10,000 in 2010, and raised the phaseout threshold from $50,000 to $60,000 for 2010;
- placed limitations on the penalty for failure to disclose reportable transactions based on resulting tax benefits;
- allowed general business credits of eligible small businesses for 2010 to be carried back five years;

---

[48] For further analysis, see CRS Report R40860, *Small Business Size Standards: A Historical Analysis of Contemporary Issues*, by Robert Jay Dilger.

- exempted general business credits of eligible small businesses in 2010 from the alternative minimum tax;
- allowed a temporary reduction in the recognition period for built-in gains tax;
- increased expensing limitations for 2010 and 2011 and allows certain real property to be treated as Section 179 property;
- allowed additional first-year depreciation for 50% of the basis of certain qualified property; and
- removed cellular telephones and similar telecommunications equipment from listed property so their cost can be deducted or depreciated like other business property.[49]

Discussion

As mentioned previously, congressional interest in the SBA's access to capital programs has increased in recent years, primarily because assisting small business in accessing capital is viewed as a means to enhance job creation and economic growth. Some, including President Obama, have argued that the SBA should be provided additional resources to assist small businesses in acquiring capital necessary to start, continue, or expand operations and create jobs.[50] Others worry about the long-term adverse economic effects of spending programs that increase the federal deficit. They also point to surveys of small business firms conducted by the National Federation of Independent Business (NFIB) which suggest that small business owners consistently place financing issues near the bottom of their most pressing concerns.[51] Instead of increasing federal funding for the SBA, they advocate small business tax reduction, reform of financial credit market regulation, and federal fiscal restraint as the best means to assist small business and foster increased levels of economic growth and job creation.[52]

Some advocates of providing additional resources to the SBA have argued that the federal government should enhance small business access to capital by creating a SBA direct lending program for small businesses.[53] During the 111th Congress, H.R. 3854, the Small Business

---

[49] For further analysis of the Small Business Jobs Act of 2010's, tax provisions, see CRS Report R41385, *Small Business Legislation During the 111th Congress*, by Robert Jay Dilger and Gary Guenther.

[50] Rep. Nydia Velázquez, "Small Business Financing and Investment Act of 2009," House debate, *Congressional Record*, daily edition, vol. 155, no. 159 (October 29, 2009), pp. H12074, H12075; Sen. Mary Landrieu, "Statements on Introduced Bills and Joint Resolutions," remarks in the Senate, *Congressional Record*, daily edition, vol. 155, no. 185 (December 10, 2009), p. S12910; and The White House, "Remarks by the President on Job Creation and Economic Growth," December 8, 2009, at http://www.whitehouse.gov/the-press-office/remarks-president-job-creation-and-economic-growth.

[51] Bruce D. Phillips and Holly Wade, Small Business Problems and Priorities (Washington, DC: NFIB Research Foundation, June 2008), p. 5, at http://www nfib.com/Portals/0/ProblemsAndPriorities08.pdf; and Holly Wade, Small Business Problems and Priorities (Washington, DC: NFIB Research Foundation, August 2012), pp. 2, 5, 14, at http://www nfib.com/research-foundation/priorities.

[52] Susan Eckerly, "NFIB Responds to President's Small Business Lending Initiatives," Washington, DC, October 21, 2009, at http://www nfib.com/newsroom/newsroom-item/cmsid/50080/; NFIB, "Government Spending," Washington, DC, at http://www nfib.com/issues-elections/issues-elections-item/cmsid/49051/; and National Federation of Independent Business, "Payroll Tax Holiday," at http://www nfib.com/issues-elections/issues-elections-item/cmsid/49039/.

[53] U.S. Congress, House Committee on Small Business, *Small Business Financing and Investment Act of 2009*, (continued...)

Financing and Investment Act of 2009, was passed by the House on October 29, 2009, by a vote of 389-32. It would have authorized a temporary SBA direct lending program.[54] Also, during the 112th Congress, H.R. 3007, the Give Credit to Main Street Act of 2011, introduced on September 21, 2011, and referred to the House Committee on Small Business, would have authorized the SBA to provide direct loans to small businesses that have been in operation as a small business for at least two years prior to its application for a direct loan. The maximum loan amount would have been the lesser of 10% of the firm's annual revenues or $500,000. Also, H.R. 5835, the Veterans Access to Capital Act of 2012, introduced on May 18, 2012, and referred to the House Committee on Small Business, would have authorized the SBA to provide up to 20% of the annual amount available for guaranteed loans under the 7(a) and 504/CDC loan guaranty programs, respectively, in direct loans to veteran-owned and -controlled small businesses.

During the 113th Congress, H.R. 2451, the Strengthening Entrepreneurs' Economic Development Act of 2013, introduced on June 20, 2013, and referred to the House Committee on Small Business, would authorize the SBA to establish a direct lending program for small businesses that have less than 20 employees. Under the bill, each loan would be limited to $150,000 and have a term of six years or less. Before issuing a direct loan, the SBA would be required to make the loan available to eligible lenders within 50 miles of the applicant's principal office. If no local lenders agree to originate, underwrite, close, and service the loan within five business days, the SBA would make the loan available to lenders in the Preferred Lender program. If still no lenders agree to originate, underwrite, close, and service the loan, the SBA shall, within 10 business days, consider the application for a direct loan.

The SBA has authority to make direct loans, both for disaster relief and for business purposes. The SBA limited the eligibility for direct business loans in 1984, 1994, and 1996 as a means to reduce costs. Until October 1, 1985, the SBA provided direct business loans to qualified small businesses. From October 1, 1985, to September 30, 1994, SBA direct business loan eligibility was limited to qualified small businesses owned by individuals with low income or located in an area of high unemployment, owned by Vietnam-era or disabled veterans, owned by the handicapped or certain organizations employing them, or certified under the minority small business capital ownership development program. Microloan program intermediaries were also eligible.[55] On October 1, 1994, SBA direct loan eligibility was limited to Microloan program intermediaries and to small businesses owned by the handicapped. Funding to support direct loans to the handicapped through the Handicapped Assistance (renamed the Disabled Assistance) Loan program ended in 1996. The last loan issued under the Disabled Assistance Loan program took place in FY1998.[56] The SBA currently offers direct business loans only to Microloan program intermediaries.

(...continued)
committee print, 111th Cong., 1st sess., October 26, 2009, H.Rept. 111-315 (Washington: GPO, 2009), pp. 13-20, 26, 27.

[54] H.R. 3854, the Small Business Financing and Investment Act of 2009 (111th Congress), §111. Capital Backstop Program.

[55] U.S. Congress, House Committee on Small Business, *Summary of Activities*, 103rd Cong., 2nd sess., January 2, 1995, H.Rept. 103-885 (Washington: GPO, 1995), p. 8; and U.S. Congress, Senate Committee on Small Business, *Hearing on the Proposed Fiscal Year 1995 Budget for the Small Business Administration*, 103rd Cong., 2nd sess., February 22, 1994, S. Hrg. 103-583 (Washington: GPO, 1994), p. 20.

[56] U.S. Congress, House Committee on Small Business, *Summary of Activities*, 105rd Cong., 2nd sess., January 2, 1999, H.Rept. 105-849 (Washington: GPO, 1999), p. 8.

Advocates for a small business direct lending program have argued that such a program would provide "rapid access to much-needed capital without having to face the administrative delays posed by the current Small Business Administration lending process."[57] Advocates of a temporary SBA direct lending program argued that such a program was necessary during periods of economic difficulty because

> In prosperous times, small businesses are able to shop around to different lenders to find the best available terms and conditions for a loan. But in times of economic downturns, those same lenders aren't as willing to lend to small businesses. More than ever during these times, it's the government's responsibility to step in to help small businesses access the loans they need to keep their businesses running and workers employed.[58]

Opponents of a small business direct lending program argue that the SBA's mission is to augment the private sector by guaranteeing loans, not compete with it by providing direct loans to small businesses.[59] They also argue that these loans hold greater risk than most; otherwise the private sector would accept them. They worry that SBA defaults may increase, resulting in added expense, either to taxpayers in the form of additional appropriations or to other small business borrowers in the form of higher fees, to cover the defaults.[60] They argue that the SBA stopped offering direct loans in 1995, primarily because the subsidy rate was "10 to 15 times higher than that of our guaranty programs."[61] They also assert that providing direct loans to small businesses might invite corruption. They note that the Reconstruction Finance Corporation (RFC), the SBA's predecessor, made direct loans to business and was accused of awarding loans based on the applicant's political connections or personal ties with RFC loan officers.[62] Opponents also argue that the SBA does not have the human, physical, and technical resources to make direct loans.

Still others argue that providing additional funding for SBA programs is largely a symbolic gesture because the SBA's guaranteed loan programs account for a relatively small fraction of small business lending.[63] They argue that, in a typical year, no more than 1% of small businesses

---

[57] Dan Gerstein, "Big Stimulus For Small Business, A new direct lending program would benefit millions," *Forbes.com*, January 14, 2009; Sharon McLoone, "Landrieu: Small Business to Benefit from Economic Plan," *The Washington Post*, February 6, 2009; George Dooley, "ASTA Renews Call For SBA Direct Lending Program," American Society of Travel Agents, Washington, DC, February 18, 2009; and Anne Kim, Ryan McConaghy, and Tess Stovall, "Federal Direct Loans to Small Businesses," *Third Way Idea Brief*, Washington, DC, April 2009.

[58] Anne Kim, Ryan McConaghy, and Tess Stovall, "Federal Direct Loans to Small Businesses," *Third Way Idea Brief*, Washington, DC, April 2009.

[59] Sue Malone, *Myth: The SBA will make direct loans under the stimulus bill*, Strategies For Small Business, Danville, CA, March 12, 2009.

[60] Representative Jeff Flake, "Providing for Consideration of H.R. 3854, Small Business Financing and Investment Act of 2009," House debate, *Congressional Record*, daily edition, vol. 155, no. 159 (October 29, 2009), pp. H12070, H 12072.

[61] U.S. Congress, Senate Committee on Small Business, *Hearing on the Proposed Fiscal Year 1995 Budget for the Small Business Administration*, 103rd Cong., 2nd sess., February 22, 1994, S. Hrg. 103-583 (Washington: GPO, 1994), p. 20.

[62] Representative Jeff Flake, "Providing for Consideration of H.R. 3854, Small Business Financing and Investment Act of 2009," House debate, *Congressional Record*, daily edition, vol. 155, no. 159 (October 29, 2009), pp. H12070, H 12072.

[63] U.S. Congress, Senate Committee on Homeland Security and Governmental Affairs, Subcommittee on Federal Financial Management, Government Information, Federal Services, and International Security, *The Effectiveness of the Small Business Administration*, 109th Cong., 2nd sess., April 6, 2006, S. Hrg. 109-492 (Washington: GPO, 2006), p. 92; and Discover Financial Services, "Discover® Small Business WatchSM: Small Business Economic Outlook Remains Cautious," Riverwoods, IL, October 26, 2009, at http://investorrelations.discoverfinancial.com/phoenix.zhtml?c=
(continued...)

receive an SBA-guaranteed loan, and those loans account for less than 3% or 4% of the total amount loaned to small businesses.[64] They assert that "these numbers show that the private banking system finances most loans and that the SBA is therefore largely irrelevant in the capital market."[65]

SBA Funding

As mentioned previously, some, including President Obama, have argued that the SBA should be provided additional funding to assist small businesses in acquiring capital necessary to start, continue, or expand operations and create jobs. Others worry about the long-term adverse economic effects of spending programs that increase the federal deficit. They advocate fiscal restraint as the best means to assist small business and foster increased levels of economic growth and job creation.

Both of these views have been reflected in recent SBA budget discussions as Congress has focused on ways to reduce the SBA's budget while not compromising the SBA's ability to assist small businesses access capital and assist individuals and businesses of all sizes cope with damages caused by natural disasters. For example, the Obama Administration had requested that the SBA be provided $968.8 million in FY2014: $191.9 million for the SBA's disaster loan programs, $111.6 million for business loan credit subsidies, and $665.3 million for all other SBA programs ($485.9 million for salaries and expenses, including $210.3 million for non-credit programs, such as SCORE, Small Business Development Centers, and Women Business Centers; $151.6 million for administrative expenses related to the SBA's business loan programs; and $27.8 million for all other SBA programs).[66]

As shown in **Table 3**, the SBA's FY2014 appropriation is $928.9 million, which is $39.9 million less than the Administration's request and significantly less than the SBA's FY2013 appropriation of $1,849.3 million ($1,754.5 million after sequestration and a required across-the-board 0.2% funding reduction). Of note, the SBA's FY2013 appropriation included $805 million in supplemental funding for disaster assistance related to Hurricane Sandy. After taking into account funding for disaster assistance and business loan subsidy costs, the SBA's FY2014 appropriation for all other programs ($625.4 million) is $41.8 million more than its FY2013 appropriation for all other programs ($583.6 million).

Table 3 also shows that the SBA's FY2014 appropriation includes $191.9 million for the SBA's disaster loan programs, $111.6 million for business loan credit subsidies, and $625.4 million for all other SBA programs ($446.1 million for salaries and expenses, including $196.1 million for

---

(...continued)

204177&p=irol-newsArticle&ID=1346088&highlight=.

[64] Raymond J. Keating, "Keating: Obama's policies will hurt, not help," *Long Island Business News, The Debate Room*, October 30, 2009, at http://libn.com/thedebateroom/2009/10/30/keating-obama%e2%80%99s-policies-will-hurt-not-help/.

[65] U.S. Congress, Senate Committee on Homeland Security and Governmental Affairs, Subcommittee on Federal Financial Management, Government Information, Federal Services, and International Security, *The Effectiveness of the Small Business Administration*, 109th Cong., 2nd sess., April 6, 2006, S.Hrg. 109-492 (Washington: GPO, 2006), p. 92.

[66] U.S. Small Business Administration, *FY2014 Congressional Budget Justification and FY2012 Annual Performance Report*, pp. 17, 22.

non-credit programs, such as SCORE, Small Business Development Centers, and Women Business Centers; $151.5 million for administrative expenses related to the SBA's business loan programs; and $27.8 million for all other SBA programs)

Table 3. Small Business Administration Funding, FY2000-FY2014

(new budget authority, in $ millions)

FY	Disaster Assistance	Business Loan Guarantee Credit Subsidies	Other Programs	Disaster Assistance, Credit Subsidies, and Other Programs Combined	Temporary, Additional Funding	Total Funding
FY2014	$191.9	$111.6	$625.4	$928.9	NA	$928.9
FY2013a	$851.2	$319.7	$583.6	$1,754.5	NA	$1,754.5
FY2012	$117.3	$210.8	$590.7	$918.8	NA	$918.8
FY2011	$45.4	$82.8	$601.5	$729.7	NA	$729.7b
FY2010	$78.2	$83.0	$662.8	$824.0	$962.5c	$1,786.5
FY2009	$0.0d	$2.5	$612.7	$615.2	$730.0e	$1,345.2
FY2008	$1,052.8	$2.0	$579.9	$1,634.7	NA	$1,634.7
FY2007	$114.9	$1.3	$455.6	$571.8	NA	$571.8
FY2006	$1,700.0	$1.3	$532.1	$2,233.4	NA	$2,233.4
FY2005	$1,042.2	$1.5	$496.5	$1,540.2	NA	$1,540.2
FY2004	$200.6	$81.0	$504.6	$786.2	NA	$786.2
FY2003	$191.5	$89.1	$505.7	$786.3	NA	$786.3
FY2002	$337.9	$0.0	$580.1	$918.0	NA	$918.0
FY2001	$284.5	$163.2	$551.8	$999.5	NA	$999.5
FY2000	$287.4	$137.8	$480.8	$906.0	NA	$906.0

Sources: U.S. Small Business Administration, Congressional Budget Justification, various years, at http://www.sba.gov/about-sba-services/217; P.L. 112-10, the Department of Defense and Full-Year Continuing Appropriations Act, 2011; P.L. 112-74, the Consolidated Appropriations Act, 2012, P.L. 112-175, the Continuing Appropriations Resolution, 2013; P.L. 113-2, the Disaster Relief Appropriations Act, 2013; P.L. 113-6, the Consolidated and Further Continuing Appropriations Act, 2013 U.S. Office of Management and Budget, *OMB Final Sequestration Report to the President and Congress for Fiscal Year 2013*; and P.L. 113-76, the Consolidated Appropriations Act, 2014.

a. Prior to sequestration and an across-the-board 0.2% funding reduction, funding for FY2013 was $896.3 million for disaster assistance, $337.3 million for business loan credit subsidies, $615.7 million for other programs, and $1,849.3 million for total funding.

b. The SBA's FY2011 appropriation of $731,201,000 ($45.5 million for SBA disaster assistance and $685.7 million for other SBA programs) was reduced to $729,738,000 by a 0.2% across-the-board rescission imposed on most appropriations accounts by P.L. 112-10, the Department of Defense and Full-Year Continuing Appropriations Act, 2011.

c. $775.0 million in temporary funding for 7(a) and 504/CDC loan guaranty program fee subsidies and loan modifications, and $187.5 million for other SBA programs. P.L. 111-118, the Department of Defense Appropriations Act, 2010, provided $125 million, P.L. 111-144, the Temporary Extension Act of 2010, provided $60 million, P.L. 111-157, the Continuing Extension Act of 2010, provided $80 million, and P.L. 111-240, the Small Business Jobs and Credit Act of 2010, provided $510 million to provide temporary fee subsidies for the SBA's 7(a) and 504/CDC loan guaranty programs and to temporarily increase the 7(a) program's maximum loan guaranty percentage to 90%. P.L. 111-240 extended the subsidies and 90% loan guaranty through December 31, 2010, and provides $187.5 million for other SBA programs that are to remain available through FY2011. Also, P.L. 111-150, to permit the use of previously appropriated funds to extend the Small Business Loan Guarantee Program, authorized the SBA to use $40 million in previously appropriated funds for fee subsidies and the 7(a) loan modification.

d. SBA disaster assistance funding in FY2009 was carried over from the previous fiscal year.

e. P.L. 111-5, the American Recovery and Reinvestment Act of 2009, provided $730 million for SBA programs, including $375 million for loan subsidies and loan modifications for the 7(a) and 504/CDC programs and $255 million for a new, temporary small business stabilization program, later named the America's Recovery Capital (ARC) Loan program.

Concluding Observations

Congress approved many changes during the 111th Congress to enhance small business access to capital. For example, P.L. 111-240, the Small Business Jobs Act of 2010, authorized the Secretary of the Treasury to establish a $30 billion Small Business Lending Fund (SBLF) to make capital investments in eligible community banks with total assets equal to or less than $1 billion or $10 billion ($4 billion was issued).[67] It authorized a $1.5 billion State Small Business Credit Initiative Program to be administered by the Department of the Treasury.[68] It made numerous changes to SBA programs in an attempt to make them more accessible to small businesses, such as increasing maximum loan amounts, creating an alternative size standard so more businesses can qualify for assistance, waiving some matching requirements, and temporarily expanding refinancing options under the 504/CDC program. It provided funding to extend SBA fee subsidies and the 7(a) program's 90% maximum loan guaranty percentage, made several changes to federal contracting law to increase small business opportunities in federal contracting, and provided about $12 billion in tax relief for small businesses. In addition, Congress approved legislation to temporarily reduce, for calendar years 2011 and 2012, payroll taxes by two percentage points for workers (including self-employed small business owners) who pay into Social Security.[69] The NFIB has long advocated a reduction of federal payroll taxes as a means to reduce small business expenses.[70]

During the 112th Congress, many bills were introduced to enhance small business access to capital, including bills to extend the SBA's temporary fee subsidies and increase the 7(a) program's loan guaranty percentage to 90%.[71] Congress did not adopt legislation that directly affected the SBA's access to capital programs. Instead, it passed legislation designed to enhance small business contracting opportunities, expand access to the SBA's surety bond guarantee program, amend the SBA's size standard practices, require a review and reassessment of the federal procurement small business goaling program, and expand small business mentor-protégé

---

[67] P.L. 111-240, the Small Business Jobs Act of 2010, §4103. Small Business Lending Fund.

[68] For further analysis see CRS Report R41385, *Small Business Legislation During the 111th Congress*, by Robert Jay Dilger and Gary Guenther.

[69] P.L. 111-312, the Tax Relief, Unemployment Insurance Reauthorization, and Job Creation Act of 2010, temporarily reduced the payroll tax by two percentage points for calendar year 2011. P.L. 112-78, the Temporary Payroll Tax Cut Continuation Act of 2011, extended the two percentage point payroll tax reduction through the first two months of 2012. P.L. 112-96, the Middle Class Tax Relief and Job Creation Act of 2012, extended the two percentage point payroll tax reduction through the end of calendar year 2012.

[70] National Federation of Independent Business, "Payroll Tax Holiday," Washington, DC, at http://www.nfib.com/issues-elections/issues-elections-item/cmsid/49039/; and National Federation of Independent Business, "Tax Package Compromise Represents a Big Victory for Small Business," Washington, DC, at http://www.nfib.com/issues-elections/issues-elections-item?cmsid=55506.

[71] For example, see H.R. 5851, the Increasing Small Business Lending Act of 2012 (112th Congress); and S. 1828, the Increasing Small Business Lending Act of 2011 (112th Congress).

programs.[72] Also, as mentioned previously, P.L. 113-76, the Consolidated Appropriations Act, 2014, increased the annual authorization amount for the SBA's SBIC program to $4 billion from $3 billion.

The question before the 113th Congress is what, if any, additional action should the federal government take to enhance small business access to capital? Should Congress decide to take further action, three not necessarily mutually exclusive options are readily apparent.

First, Congress could adopt a wait-and-see strategy that focuses on congressional oversight of the programmatic changes to the SBA's programs that have been enacted during the 111th, 112th, and 113th Congresses. Advocates of this approach could argue that small business credit markets have generally improved over the past two years, the SBA's lending has stabilized at pre-recession levels, and the demand for small business loans is increasing. Therefore, it could be argued that evaluating the impact of the programmatic changes to the SBA's programs that have been enacted over the past several years, especially given that economic conditions appear to be improving, should take place before taking further congressional action to improve small business access to capital.

Second, Congress could consider additional changes to the SBA's programs in an effort to enhance small business access to capital, such as considering a direct lending program, providing additional funding for SBA fee subsidies and loan modifications, or increasing funding for SBA programs. For example, during the 111th Congress, S. 3967, the Small Business Investment and Innovation Act of 2010, would have authorized funding increases for the SBA's training and technical assistance programs, established a Rural Small Business Technology Pilot Program, increased maximum loan limits for the SBA's home and business disaster loan programs, increased surety bond limits, and expanded eligibility for the SBA's State Trade and Export Promotion Grant Program to cities and other major metropolitan areas. Advocates of this approach could argue that although small business credit markets have generally improved over the past two years, job growth is still a concern. In their view, assisting small businesses access capital would help to create and retain jobs.

Third, Congress could consider the repeal of portions of the Small Business Jobs Act of 2010, or other SBA programs. For example, on March 15, 2011, the House Committee on Small Business approved its views and estimates for the concurrent resolution on the budget for FY2012. The committee recommended that the SBA's budget be "cut nearly $100 million."[73] The committee recommended that 14 programs, including several management and technical assistance training programs, be defunded "because they duplicate existing programs at the SBA or at other agencies" or "where there is an absence of any evidence that they will help small businesses create new jobs."[74] In its views and estimates letter for the FY2013 budget, the House Committee on Small Business recommended, on March 7, 2012, that funding be reduced for several SBA

---

[72] P.L. 112-239, the National Defense Authorization Act for Fiscal Year 2013.

[73] Representative Sam Graves, "Opening Statement for Views and Estimates Markup," Washington, DC, March 15, 2011, at http://www.smallbusiness.house.gov/Calendar/EventSingle.aspx?EventID=227626.

[74] Ibid. For further information concerning the funding recommendations contained in the House Committee on Small Business views and estimates for the concurrent resolution on the budget for FY2012 see U.S. Congress, House Committee on Small Business, "Views and Estimates of the Committee on Small Business on Matters to be set forth in the Concurrent Resolution on the Budget for FY2012, communication to the Chairman, House Committee on the Budget," 112th Cong., 1st sess., March 17, 2011, at http://smbiz.house.gov/UploadedFiles/March_17_Views_and_Estimates_Letter.pdf.

programs, including funding for 7(j) technical assistance, microloan technical assistance, and the National Women's Business Council. It also recommended that funding be eliminated for Women's Business Centers, Veterans Business Centers, Prime Technical Assistance, HUBZone outreach, the Office of Native American Affairs, and the Office of International Trade. It also recommended that funding be eliminated for several SBA initiatives, including the Drug-Free Workplace, Clusters, and National Veterans Entrepreneurial Training Program.[75]

Advocates of this option argue that instead of increasing federal funding for the SBA, the federal government should focus on small business tax reduction and federal fiscal restraint as the best means to assist small business and foster increased levels of economic growth and job creation.[76]

---

[75] U.S. Congress, House Committee on Small Business, "Views and Estimates of the Committee on Small Business on Matters to be set forth in the Concurrent Resolution on the Budget for FY2013, communication to the Chairman, House Committee on the Budget," 112th Cong., 1st sess., March 7, 2012 at http://smallbusiness.house.gov/uploadedfiles/views_and_estimates_fy_2013.pdf.

[76] Susan Eckerly, "NFIB Responds to President's Small Business Lending Initiatives," Washington, DC, October 21, 2009, at http://www.nfib.com/newsroom/newsroom-item/cmsid/50080/; NFIB, "Government Spending," Washington, DC, at http://www.nfib.com/issues-elections/issues-elections-item/cmsid/49051/; and National Federation of Independent Business, "Payroll Tax Holiday," at http://www.nfib.com/issues-elections/issues-elections-item/cmsid/49039/.

Appendix. Selected Provisions in the Small Business Jobs Act of 2010

Table A-1. Selected Provisions, the Small Business Jobs Act of 2010

Issue/Program	The Small Business Jobs Act of 2010
SBA 7(a) Program	increased the 7(a) Program's loan limit from $2 million to $5 million.
SBA 504 Program	increased the 504/CDC Program's loan limits from $1.5 million to $5 million for "regular" borrowers, from $2 million to $5 million if the loan proceeds are directed toward one or more specified public policy goals, and from $4 million to $5.5 million for manufacturers; and temporarily expanded for two years the eligibility for low-interest refinancing under the SBA's 504/CDC program for qualified debt.
SBA Express Program	temporarily increased for one year the Express Program's loan limit from $350,000 to $1 million (expired on September 26, 2011).
SBA Microloan Program	increased the Microloan Program's loan limit for borrowers from $35,000 to $50,000; and increased the loan limits for Microloan intermediaries after their first year in the program from $3.5 million to $5 million.
Temporary SBA fee subsidies and loan modifications	temporarily increased the SBA's guaranty on 7(a) loans to 90% and provided for the elimination of selected fees on the SBA's 7(a) and 504 loans through December 31, 2010.
SBA secondary market	extended the SBA's secondary market lending authority under ARRA from 2 years from enactment to 2 years from the first sale of a pool of first lien position 504 loans guaranteed under this authority investor (which took place on September 24, 2010).
SBA size standards	authorized the SBA to establish an alternative size standard for the SBA's 7(a) and 504 programs that would use maximum tangible net worth and average net income; and to established an interim alternative size standard of not more than $15 million in tangible net worth and not more than $2 million in average net income for the two full fiscal years before the date of the application.
SBA International Trade Finance Program	increased the International Trade Finance Program's loan limit from $1.75 million, of which not more than $1.25 million may be used for working capital, supplies, or financings, to $4.5 million.
State Trade and Export Promotion Grant Program	established an associate administrator for the SBA's Office of International Trade and a state trade and export promotion grant program.

Issue/Program	The Small Business Jobs Act of 2010
Federal contracting	imposed contract bundling accountability measures directing federal agencies to include in each solicitation for any contract award above the agency's substantial bundling threshold a provision soliciting bids by small business teams and joint ventures;
	required federal agencies to publish on its website its policy on contract bundling and consolidation, as well as a rationale for any bundled contract solicited or awarded;
	repealed the small business competitiveness demonstration program; and
	provided parity among the small business contracting programs (including striking "shall" and inserting "may" in 15 U.S.C. 657a(b)(2)(B), which refers to the agency's discretion to provide contracting preference to HUBZone small businesses).
Small Business Lending Fund	authorized the U.S. Treasury to make up to $30 billion of capital investments ($4 billion was issued);
	CBO estimated the program would raise $1.1 billion over 10 years.
State Small Business Credit Initiative Program	authorized $1.5 billion for the State Small Business Credit Initiative Program.
SBA Intermediary Lending Pilot Program	authorized a three-year Intermediary Lending Pilot Program to allow the SBA to make direct loans to not more than 20 eligible nonprofit lending intermediaries each year totaling not more than $20 million. The intermediaries, in turn, would be allowed to make loans to new or growing small businesses, not to exceed $200,000 per business.
Capital gains taxation	temporarily raised to 100% the exclusion of gains on certain small business stock from enactment to end of calendar year.
Limitation on penalties for failure to disclose reportable transactions	placed limitations on the penalty for failure to disclose reportable transactions based on resulting tax benefits.
Deduction for start-up expenditures	increased the deduction for qualified start-up expenditures from $5,000 to $10,000 in 2010, and the phaseout threshold from $50,000 to $60,000 for 2010.
Business carry back	allowed general business credits of eligible small businesses for 2010 to be carried back 5 years.
Alternative Minimum Tax	exempted general business credits of eligible small businesses in 2010 from the alternative minimum tax.
Recognition period for built-In gains tax	allowed a temporary reduction in the recognition period for built-in gains tax.
Expensing and Section 179 property	increased expensing limitations for 2010 and 2011; and allowed certain real property to be treated as Section 179 property.
Depreciation	allowed additional first-year depreciation for 50% of the basis of certain qualified property.
Deduction for health insurance costs	allowed the deduction for health insurance costs in computing self-employment taxes in 2010.

Issue/Program	The Small Business Jobs Act of 2010
Deduction for cellular telephones	removed cellular telephones and similar telecommunications equipment from listed property so their cost can be deducted or depreciated like other business property.
Crude tall oil	made crude tall oil ineligible for the cellulosic biofuel producer credit.
Section 561 of the Hiring Incentives to Restore Employment Act	increased the percentage under Section 561 of the Hiring Incentives to Restore Employment Act by 36 percentage points.
Rental income reporting	required taxpayers that receive rental income from leasing real property to file information returns to the IRS and to service providers that report receiving payments of $600 or more during the tax year for rental property expenses (repealed by P.L. 112-9, the Comprehensive 1099 Taxpayer Protection and Repayment of Exchange Subsidy Overpayments Act of 2011).
Penalties for failing to file information returns to the IRS	increased the penalties for failing to file information returns to the IRS and to payees in a timely manner.
Treasury Department authority to apply a continuous levy on federal contractors	expanded the Treasury Department's authority to apply a continuous levy to government payments to federal contractors that owe the IRS for unpaid taxes to include payments for property such as a new office building. Current law allows the levy to be applied to payments for goods and services only.
Predictive modeling to identify Medicaid waste, fraud, and abuse	authorized the use of predictive modeling to identify and prevent waste, fraud, and abuse in the Medicare fee-for-service program.
Roth Retirement Accounts	allowed participants in government Section 457 plans to treat elective deferrals as Roth contributions; and
	allowed rollovers from elective deferral plans to designated Roth accounts.
Nonqualified annuities	allowed holders of nonqualified annuities (i.e., annuity contracts held outside of a tax-qualified retirement plan or IRA) to elect to receive a portion of the contract in the form of a stream of annuity contracts, leaving the remainder of the contract to accumulate income on a tax-deferred basis.

Source: P.L. 111-240, the Small Business Jobs Act of 2010.

Author Contact Information

Robert Jay Dilger
Senior Specialist in American National Government
rdilger@crs.loc.gov, 7-3110

www.ingramcontent.com/pod-product-compliance
Lightning Source LLC
Chambersburg PA
CBHW081809170526
45167CB00008B/3391